riot

ANDREW MOODIE

Riot
first published 1997 by
Scirocco Drama
An imprint of J. Gordon Shillingford Publishing Inc.
© 1996 Andrew Moodie
Reprinted 1999, 2002, 2016

Scirocco Drama Editor: Dave Carley
Cover design by Terry Gallagher/Doowah Design Inc.
Cover photos by Kevin Pickles
Author photo by Sheilagh Corbett
Printed and bound in Canada

We acknowledge the financial support of the Manitoba Arts Council and The Canada
Council for the Arts for our publishing program.

Canadian Cataloguing in Publication Data

Moodie, Andrew, 1967-
    Riot

ISBN 1-896239-20-X

    I. Title.

PS8576.O558R56 1997   C812'.54   C97-9900088-2
PR9199.3.M598R56 1997

J. Gordon Shillingford Publishing
P.O. Box 86, 905 Corydon Avenue, Winnipeg, MB Canada R3M 3S3

*Dedicated to every ambitious
young Canadian black actor.*

This play is for you. Have fun.

Acknowledgements

Many thanks to Andy Moro, Neil Foster, Michael Springate, Rebecca Cann, Fiona Reid, Dian English, Taulene Ayoub, Layne Coleman, Gina Madahbee, Don, Bryan James, David James, Richard Yearwood, Mom, Dad, Beaner, Melanie Nicholls-King, Tanya Laffin, Cara Hostetler, Crystal Mulock, Sam Norton, Jonathan Rooke, Ontario Arts Council, Toronto Arts Council, Stephan Droege, Sharon Lewis, John-Kelley Cuthbertson, Tim Hill, Ian Hutson, Annette Kraft, Van Ermel, Ed Roy, Gabriella Caruso, Lisa Ruelling, Kirstin Halliwell, Chris Sproule, Catherine Bruhier, Maxine Bailey, Conrad Coates, Louis Taylor, George Seremba, Welcome Ngozi, and Karen Robinson.

Andrew Moodie

Andrew Moodie is an Ottawa-born and raised actor, with extensive stage, film and television credits. *Riot*, his first play (Scirocco, 1997), was an immediate success with critics and audiences after premiering in 1995 at Toronto's Factory Theatre. It was subsequently remounted at the 1996 du Maurier World Stage Festival in Toronto, and produced at Ottawa's Great Canadian Theatre Company, Montreal's Monument Nationale by Black Theatre Workshop, and Halifax's Neptune Theatre. It won the 1996 Chalmers Canadian Play Award. Andrew's second play, *Oui*, premiered at Toronto's Factory Theatre in 1998. His third play, *A Common Man's Guide to Loving Women* (Scirocco, 1999) premiered in 1999 at Ottawa's National Arts Centre (in a coproduction with the Canadian Stage Company).

Characters

WENDLE, a student, 20s, from Halifax, Nova Scotia
ALEX, a student, 20s, from Ottawa
HENRY, owner of electrical repair company, 30s, from Uganda
KIRK, a student, late teens, from Kingston, Jamaica
EFFIE, a student, 20s, from Vancouver
GRACE, a student, 20s, born in Jamaica and raised in Montreal, Kirk's sister

Setting

A house in Toronto, 1992

Stage left: Door leading to the backyard
Down stage left: Dining area, dining table. On the table is a cordless phone receiver.
Up stage left: Door leading to the kitchen. Desk with a computer. Bookshelf.
Up stage centre: Stairs leading to the second and third floors.
Centre stage: Couch, chairs. TV set on a milk crate. VCR.
Stage right: Stereo and front door.

Production Credits

Riot premiered on October 5, 1995, at the Factory Theatre,
Toronto, Canada, with the following cast:

EFFIE... Catherine Bruhier
WENDLE..Conrad Coates
ALEX..Andrew Moodie
GRACE ....Karen Robinson
HENRY .... George Seremba
KIRK... Richard Yearwood

Directed by Layne Coleman
Set and lighting design by Stephan Droege
Sound design by Andy Moro
Assistant Director: Sharon M. Lewis
Stage Manager: Bryan James

Playwright's Notes

Watch the pace. The play is dialogue heavy. Don't hurry the delivery, but definitely come in with your line on time. There are plenty of silences in the stage directions. If too many silences are added, the pace goes. I have listed a few warnings that will help to keep you clear of certain pitfalls.

ALEX: Alex is just discovering his sexuality; if you play him too gay then the audience will wonder why Effie went out with him and why Kirk can't figure it out. By all means, play around with the character, but be careful. The line, "He's in his sexual prime" is meant to be ironic.

HENRY: In much of the beginning of the play, I have left Henry doing nothing. Just sitting around. The first actor who played Henry chose to talk on his cellphone and make important deals. It worked great. You can do that, or read, or make some food. Anything. Have fun.

GRACE: The 'Critical Mother Figure' thing is a trap. Keep a close eye on her vulnerabilities. Don't forget her deep love for Kirk is in her actions, but not always her words.

WENDLE: Wendle is frustrated. He gets angry when his frustration cannot find release. There are many different ways to approach his frustration; perhaps there is a lot of clinical pragmatist in Wendle, perhaps more fun-loving jokester who sees himself as brave altruist. I don't know. You make it up but watch out for the anger trap.

EFFIE: Playing the slut/bimbo is a trap. Keep an eye on her complexity, intelligence and strength. In the play-fighting scene with Kirk feel free to play with him. The dialogue is based on a wonderful improvisation that happened in rehearsal. Don't let it get too choreographed or rehearsed. Both you and Kirk are free to surprise each other, with two rules a) don't hurt yourselves, and b) the kiss should come out of nowhere.

KIRK: The song Kirk sings for his sister—feel free to improvise any dub poetry you want, to lead into the song and give it a real Jamaican dance hall feel. One restriction: don't go over thirty seconds for the whole song. And finally, yes he stole, yes he has a gun, yes he has incredible rage, but he also has a lot of joy.

The last half of the play has numerous speeches. These speeches are meant to give each character a chance to express something intimate. This places a considerable amount of the pace and direction of the play in your hands. My one word of advice: command the stage. It's yours. Don't look at the speeches as something to get through. Look at it as your time to shine. And most of all, have fun. Don't step off the stage feeling that you've done it right. Come off the stage having enjoyed yourself. The text is dependent on it.

Player's Manifesto

Acting is the art of behavioural signifiers. It is an art, but it is also a craft. For example, everyone must eat. Preparing food is essential to every living thing, but in the hands of some, it is an art. Behaviour is essential to every living thing. It warns others of danger, it tells whether a stranger is a threat, it communicates detailed information about things unseen, it distracts and entertains. Behaviour is both learned and innate. It is something we are all intimately familiar with and yet still mystified by. Those of us whose lives are dedicated to the art of performing behaviour before others participate in something called Play. Gregory Bateson in his *Theory of Play and Fantasy* notes that behaviour that carries the statement "This is play" contains a paradoxical message of "These actions in which we now engage do not denote what those actions *for which they stand* would denote." In other words, the behaviour that is witnessed, is not the behaviour *for which it stands*. It is behaviour that signifies.

A play can come into being in many ways. It can be created collectively, it can be improvised, it can be written. A playwright is an artist who encodes a blank piece of paper with text. This text is then given to the actor who in turn decodes the text, interprets it and then performs it. The communication begins with the playwright, but then is entrusted to an actor. The actor interprets the text, and in turn the behaviour suggested by the text. There are many different techniques, from many different ages and parts of the world. Some believe that certain techniques from certain countries, or certain ages are superior to another. The writer doesn't really care. The writer only knows the text they have created, and that they want to see the behaviour they encoded brought to life with strident verisimilitude and vitality. They want the actor to join them on an arduous, quasi-empirical, mystical exploration of this animal we call the human being.

Act I

(Lights come up on stage to reveal GRACE at the dining table studying. EFFIE is on the couch, wrapped in a blanket, watching TV, eating Doritos. EFFIE slowly stands, points the remote control at the TV. The lights and music fade.)

WENDLE: Fuck Quebec!

(Lights up. The table is cluttered with their text and note books. EFFIE is lying on the couch. The TV is off.)

GRACE: Quebec is a distinct society!

WENDLE: What the fuck makes Quebec a distinct society?!

GRACE: The French language and culture.

WENDLE: Being a black man from Nova Scotia, does that not make me distinct?

GRACE: Yes you are distinct, but that doesn't stop them from being distinct.

WENDLE: Look, you know me, I voted for Brian Mulroney, he's from Quebec. It's not that I don't like people from Quebec, it's just that when they try to tell me that they are better than me, I get pissed off.

GRACE: They're not saying they're better than you, they are looking for the tools to protect their culture.

WENDLE: Jean Chretien is French! He's from Quebec! He doesn't seem to think that we are destroying French culture.

GRACE: Look, I have friends back in Montreal who would tell you that Jean Chretien is a brown-nosing two-faced Uncle Tom opportunist who will lick English Canada's asshole so that one day he will become prime minister, okay?

WENDLE: You are seriously fucking deluded.

GRACE: I'm just telling you what some people are saying.

WENDLE: Well look, if you're French and from Quebec at least you have a shot at becoming prime minister. There ain't gonna be no black prime minister here in Canada within my lifetime and you know it.

GRACE: You got me there. Fine.

WENDLE: Maybe they should stop thinking about their own culture for a moment and think about other cultures, like what they're doing to Native people!

GRACE: Oh come on!

WENDLE: The French are the most racist, bigoted people in the world.

GRACE: Bullshit!

WENDLE: You go to those people in Oka, you go tell the Mohawks how wonderful Quebec culture is!

GRACE: Don't you dare try and tell me that the people in Quebec are so racist, but hey, Nova Scotians love Native people, Nova Scotians don't have a racist bone in their body!

WENDLE: Quebecers are more racist than people in Nova Scotia.

GRACE: You've never lived in Quebec! You have no idea...

WENDLE: They had slavery in Quebec!

GRACE: They had slavery in Nova Scotia!

WENDLE:	Okay, look, you want me to feel sympathy for Quebec, why should I feel sympathy for Quebec?
GRACE:	1804 to around 1805 there was a crop failure in Lower Canada.
WENDLE:	Here we go.
GRACE:	This lead to lumber production becoming the number one export to England. With increased export there came with it increased immigration from England. These newly-landed immigrants...
WENDLE:	Look, I don't have a problem with...
GRACE:	Just shut up and listen to me for a second!
WENDLE:	Don't tell me to...
GRACE:	These immigrants were shocked that the French played such a large role in the civil service, and the French were shocked that the English came to dominate the economy. Pierre Bédard, leader of the Canadian party, was arrested for...this is what drives me crazy about you Canadians! You should learn your own friggin' history!

(WENDLE turns to EFFIE.)

WENDLE:	I am so glad I am no longer going out with that woman, I swear to God.

(The cordless phone rings.)

EFFIE:	If it's my Mom I'm not here.
WENDLE:	Neither am I.
GRACE:	So...what, I'm supposed to answer the phone for y'all.
EFFIE:	Answer the goddamned phone.
WENDLE:	Language...

EFFIE: The fuck do you mean, "Language"! You're f-this
                and f-that...

WENDLE: You don't have to slander God, keep God out of it.

EFFIE: Don't make me get up, just don't... Grace get the
                phone!

                (She does.)

GRACE: Yo. Hello. Yes she is.

                *(EFFIE mouths,"Who is it?" GRACE hands the
                phone to her.)*

EFFIE: Hello? Hey ma.

                *(EFFIE gives GRACE the finger. GRACE blows
                her a kiss. ALEX walks in the front door and goes
                upstairs. EFFIE's line overlaps with GRACE and
                ALEX.)*

                I'm sorry. I know. How was your day?

GRACE: Get back down here.

ALEX: What did I do?

GRACE: The computer ate my paper.

ALEX: What!?

                (ALEX stops, looks at EFFIE.)

EFFIE: I'm on the rag. Oh yeah. Did you see him again?

                *(ALEX mouths "Who is she talking to?" GRACE
                mouths "Her Mom." ALEX nods. WENDLE
                leaves his room with a small plant. The rest of
                EFFIE's speech overlaps with ALEX and GRACE's
                dialogue.)*

                What did he say. Oh yeah. No. No it doesn't.
                Because I just...no. Because I know. Because in my
                little experience as a human being on this planet,

I've been there. Mom... Mom... Mom... listen to me for a sec... Mom? Yes he is. Yes he is.

GRACE: I was in WordPerfect, I imported a graphic into my paper, I workin on it not more than five minutes and boom she gone and I ready to smash de rasclot ting pon de wall.

ALEX: One more time in English please.

(WENDLE walks by her. He smiles or laughs. He goes to the backyard. GRACE pulls out a piece of scrap paper. ALEX finds it hard to keep his eyes off EFFIE.)

GRACE: It said, "Segment Load Error; A500:67907811", then it said it was going to shut down if I...if I pressed "yes" and it did.

ALEX: Either there is a problem with the microprocessor or we need more RAM.

GRACE: I want my paper back.

ALEX: Don't you have it on disk?

EFFIE: Alex.

GRACE: Not most of it. Not ten pages.

EFFIE: Alex.

ALEX: What...

EFFIE: You need to use the phone.

ALEX: What?

EFFIE: You need to use the phone.

ALEX: I need to use the phone.

EFFIE: Ma, someone needs to use the phone.

(KIRK runs in the front door and up the stairs.)

ALEX: It's a 286 processor right? And the program is supposed to be able to run on a 286 with one meg RAM, but I hear it works better on a 386 with four meg RAM.

GRACE: RAM.

EFFIE: Alex… He's fine.

ALEX: We've got two, I could try getting four or eight.

GRACE: Right.

ALEX: I thought getting the Quarter-Deck memory manager would help. It manages the 640K below the first megabyte. Now TSR programs like the mouse driver…

GRACE: I don't know what you're saying to me right now. I just want my paper back.

ALEX: Okay.

GRACE: I don't care about RAM or any of that stuff…

               (EFFIE hands the phone to ALEX. He takes the phone.)

ALEX: Hey Fiona.

GRACE: Kirk, there's a house meeting tonight…

ALEX: Go on. Anything at all, go ahead. Oh yeah. Well…he should wear a condom.

EFFIE: (For her mother to hear.) Whad I say!

               (WENDLE goes to the kitchen.)

ALEX: He should anyway. It doesn't matter… You don't know that. Because men lie sometimes.

EFFIE: HA!

ALEX: She's fine. Sorry? I think your daughter is a wonderful person. She *is* very pretty. Yes. I have to use the phone. Yes. Yes. Sorry. Okay. Nice...nice talking to you. Bye. Bye.

(He hangs up.)

EFFIE: I can't believe my Mom talked to you. That's too hilarious.

ALEX: Yes it is.

EFFIE: I mean it's just too funny.

ALEX: Now I know where you get it from.

EFFIE: Get what.

ALEX: Your theatricality.

EFFIE: So men lie, eh Alex?

ALEX: I guess they do.

EFFIE: I think there's some irony floating around somewhere.

(WENDLE returns with a peanut butter sandwich.)

ALEX: So what happened again?

GRACE: The machine ate my paper.

EFFIE: Alex? Any irony?

ALEX: When are you moving out?

EFFIE: Not soon enough.

(WENDLE sits at the table.)

WENDLE: Peanut butter sandwich anyone?

GRACE: No thanks.

ALEX: Is that my peanut butter?

WENDLE:　　No it's not your motherfucking peanut butter, shut the fuck up.

　　　　　　(EFFIE goes upstairs.)

GRACE:　　Is that it?

ALEX:　　Check it out.

　　　　　　(ALEX goes to the kitchen. There is a knock at the door.)

WENDLE:　　Who is it!

　　　　　　(ALEX looks at WENDLE, chastising him for not getting the door. HENRY enters.)

HENRY:　　Is Grace there?

GRACE:　　I'm not ready.

HENRY:　　Oh, okay.

WENDLE:　　My brother.

HENRY:　　Hey Wendle.

GRACE:　　You want to sit with Wendle for a while?

HENRY:　　Well if we want dinner, we have to leave soon.

GRACE:　　I know, I know. Sit with Wendle. This won't take too long.

HENRY:　　I didn't want to go through this again.

GRACE:　　It's something that happened with the computer...

　　　　　　(KIRK jumps down the stairs and out the door. ALEX steps out of the kitchen with a generous shot of Scotch and some ice. He leans against the couch.)

　　　　　　...today—Hey, there's a house meeting, Kirk!

　　　　　　(KIRK peeks his head back in.)

KIRK:　　What.

GRACE: There's a house meeting.

KIRK: When.

GRACE: Five minutes.

KIRK: A'ight.

> (*He runs off. EFFIE takes a few steps down the stairs and looks around, sees ALEX and goes back into her room. ALEX sees her do this and goes to the backyard.*)

HENRY: How long are you going to be?

GRACE: Just a bit longer.

HENRY: What do you mean just a bit. How long is just a bit.

GRACE: Don't start. Please do not start.

HENRY: But this always happens! Why do you always leave things to the last minute?!

GRACE: I'm sorry.

HENRY: I hate rushing around. I really do.

> (*She goes over to him and hugs him.*)

GRACE: I know I said I wouldn't do this…

HENRY: Don't talk to me right now. Just get the work done. Go. Work.

GRACE: We don't have to go out at all.

HENRY: Just go to work.

> (*She goes back to the computer.*)

WENDLE: So how you doing.

HENRY: Fine. What happened to the sound.

WENDLE: I don't know.

(*HENRY goes to the television and looks at it. He fiddles with the sound knob.*)

WENDLE: Were you here when the sound cut out... Grace?

GRACE: What?

WENDLE: Were you here when the sound cut out?

GRACE: No. Ask Effie. She knows all about it.

WENDLE: Aww, forget about it. Sit down man. Come on.

               (*He does.*)

               How you doing.

HENRY: Hard day. Hard day.

WENDLE: What.

HENRY: Nothing. Just a hard day.

               (*ALEX comes back in from the backyard, grabs a newspaper, and sits at table.*)

GRACE: Tell him.

WENDLE: Tell me what.

HENRY: I was stopped by the police.

WENDLE: No way.

HENRY: I made an illegal left turn and the guy, he comes up behind me and tells me that he just wants to look in my van.

WENDLE: You're kidding me.

HENRY: He searched my van. When I started to argue, his partner pulled out a gun and searches me. I don't know what he was looking for, but...

WENDLE: I mean what the fuck...every black man is hiding drugs in his car. Fuck! Fuck that!

ALEX: So what happened?

HENRY: Well, they searched me and I got a ticket and they left.

ALEX: Well you've got to file a complaint.

HENRY: No, no.

ALEX: You have to. Do you remember what the two cops looked like?

HENRY: Alex...I am not going to do anything.

ALEX: You have to.

HENRY: The police in this country don't scare me.

ALEX: The Metro Toronto police force is not here to scare you. You are a business person. You own a very successful electrical company. You pay your taxes, you employ Canadians, the Metro Toronto police force should at least, at the very least apologize! Am I right? They should at least say that you are a valued person in this community, and there was obviously some terrible mistake, and you should be made to feel welcome here.

WENDLE: Alex, let me tell you a story. One summer I went to live with my uncle, and out east, they've got this thing called "Broom the Coon". And what that is...a bunch of white guys get in a car late at night, they take a broom with them, and when they see a black person on the street, they step on the gas, they stick the broom out the window, and they smack him on the head.

GRACE: You're joking.

WENDLE: So, I'm walking down the street one night, going home. This car goes by, then pulls a U-ee, and when a car does that late at night, and you're black, you know you're in for it. So I run towards the car, grab the broom, start pulling, these two humongous white guys get out of the car and proceed to beat the living shit out of me. Somebody calls the station, tells the police that two white guys are being attacked by a crazed Negro with a knife. The cops arrive, take me to the station. The commanding officer? I'm all covered in bruises right? I try to tell him my story, but he doesn't want to hear it. He turns to the arresting officer, goes, "Did you get a statement." The arresting officer goes, "No." And that's it. On my record I have an assault charge. I'd contest it but it looks so good. I kicked the shit out of two white guys, single-handed.

GRACE: It's like the police are some kind of occupying army or something. You know? It's like, don't look them in the eye, don't make any sudden movements when you walk by.

ALEX: But I think that feeling is pretty universal. I mean, white people feel just as nervous around cops as we do.

GRACE: Yes, but because I'm black I feel like when I step out that door and I see a cop, my life is at risk.

WENDLE: This country is racist from top to bottom. From the police force, to the military, to the business sector, to the CBC... I mean the fuck is it with this *Road to Avonlea* shit? There's not a single black person in sight! My ancestors fucking fought and died to help found this country. They settled right next door to that part of the world. I have never seen a black face on that show!

ALEX: How the fuck do you know, you never watch the fucking program!

WENDLE: Philippe Rushton is supported by big business.

ALEX: Oh please.

WENDLE: It's true! That's why they refuse to fire him. His research helps to discourage employment equity.

ALEX: If I wanted conspiracy theories, I'd call Oliver Stone.

WENDLE: The government created the Heritage Front.

ALEX: Oh come on!

WENDLE: They did.

ALEX: Yeah, yeah.

GRACE: A friend of mine who works in the Anti-Racism League told me that CSIS started the Heritage Front and funds its rallies.

ALEX: Do you have any evidence whatsoever to back this up.

GRACE: Well my friend says…

ALEX: No, no, no, no, do you have any evidence to back this up.

GRACE: No but…

ALEX: Then how am I supposed to believe what you're saying?!

WENDLE: Because this country is run by white people and that's just the way white people are. It's in their nature. It's in their genetic make-up to try and fuck us over every opportunity they get.

ALEX: That's racist!

WENDLE: Yeah, but it's true! In the States you can fight racism because they're so open about it. That way, black people have more opportunities. Canada is ten times more racist than the States but they hide it here. Every aspect of this country is racist. They just hide it.

ALEX: Then what do you expect me to do? Do you expect
              me to live my life in fear of some unseen form
              of…of oppression or something.

WENDLE: Just open your eyes Alex. Stop living in a dream
              world.

HENRY: Maybe Madonna was right.

WENDLE: What.

HENRY: Maybe Toronto is a fascist city.

GRACE: The police won't even leave Madonna alone.
              "Damn."

WENDLE: When is this notorious house meeting?

GRACE: We should get this thing on the road. Alex!

ALEX: I'm right here.

GRACE: I mean Effie. Effie!

              (GRACE goes to the computer.)

ALEX: Hey. What happened to the sound?

              (ALEX pounces on WENDLE in an attempt to steal
              the remote. He is unsuccessful.)

WENDLE: Hey!

ALEX: The Rodney King trial is on CNN.

WENDLE: Oh right.

HENRY: Can I see the paper?

              (The newspaper is in a mess on the floor.)

ALEX: Sure man, what section?

HENRY: Entertainment.

              (ALEX gives HENRY the section. HENRY looks

over GRACE's shoulder, she motions for him to go away.)

GRACE: Did you go to any classes today?

  (No response. WENDLE taps ALEX.)

GRACE: Alex.

ALEX: What.

GRACE: Did you go to any classes today?

ALEX: No Ma.

GRACE: Just asking.

ALEX: Bite me.

GRACE: It's your life.

ALEX: And I can do what I want.

GRACE: Effie!

EFFIE: *(Offstage.)* What!

GRACE: *(With a Jamaican accent.)* House Meeting!

  (ALEX jumps off the couch.)

ALEX: Let's get this party started right!

  (WENDLE gets up, they both go to the table. EFFIE comes down the stairs and sits.)

EFFIE: Grace.

GRACE: I'm just shutting down the computer. It takes a while.

ALEX: Shouldn't Kirk be here?

GRACE: He said he'd be back.

WENDLE: Should we wait for him?

GRACE: No.

           (GRACE shuts down the computer and sits.)

           Okay.

HENRY: Guys. You might want to see this.

WENDLE: What.

HENRY: The trial.

ALEX: Is it over?

HENRY: They're just about to read the verdict.

EFFIE: Could we get this done now?

ALEX: It'll take two minutes.

EFFIE: You're going to hear it on the news anyway.

ALEX: Can we just take two minutes to watch this please.

EFFIE: Aww, come on guys. They're guilty, they're going to jail. What's there to see.

ALEX: Shhh.

EFFIE: Don't shhh me. There's no sound. What the hell do you want to shhh me for? Idiot.

           (They all stand in silence for a moment.)

HENRY: I don't understand. Is the jury reading the verdict or not.

WENDLE: I think they're doing it now.

ALEX: What just happened?

GRACE: Why are they smiling?

WENDLE: They won.

HENRY: No.

           (EFFIE joins them at the TV.)

ALEX: Yeah, I think they did.

EFFIE: No.

GRACE: Wait, wait, wait, wait, guys. Here it is.

             (On the screen, a written transcript of the jury's findings.)

WENDLE: Not guilty. Not guilty.

             (They all move away from the TV set. WENDLE goes to the kitchen. There is a twenty-five second silence.)

ALEX: Where was the trial held?

GRACE: Something valley.

EFFIE: Where were the black people on that jury?

GRACE: I didn't see any.

HENRY: I mean, what...do they not see a human being? Laying on the ground, bleeding! Being beaten to death?

GRACE: There's got to be an appeal.

EFFIE: Think so?

GRACE: They have to. I mean, come on.

ALEX: I know this isn't the best time to play devil's advocate, but...the jury was not asked if it was inhumane, they were asked if it was within the law...within police procedure.

HENRY: How can you say that beating someone like that is police procedure!

ALEX: I'm not saying it's right or wrong, I'm just saying that...yeah, the way they treated Rodney King has been police procedure, in America, for quite some time. And if it wasn't for that videotape, we wouldn't even be talking about it.

EFFIE: As a matter of fact, it took a long time for the video to even make it into the news. A lot of stations refused to play it at first.

GRACE: Shhh. They're playing the video again.

                (They watch together in silence for a while. They react to the video.)

ALEX: Okay, now…someone shows that to the jury and says, "Look, you're a cop. An L.A. cop. You don't know if he's on crack, PCP, whatever. You don't want him to get your gun…"

WENDLE: That's a black man Alex.

ALEX: I know.

WENDLE: This is what they do to keep us down. To keep you down. To keep me down.

ALEX: Okay.

WENDLE: I swear to God I try not to hate white people. I swear to God I try to turn the other cheek, but as the God I love is my witness, I only have so many cheeks. And I swear by the Lord that I love, they will not treat me like an animal. But they turn around and do something like this and you can't do anything. You can't do anything. I mean…

                (WENDLE exits. KIRK runs in the front door as WENDLE runs out.)

KIRK: What's the matter with him.

EFFIE: The guys who attacked Rodney King got off.

KIRK: No.

                (GRACE goes outside to see about WENDLE.)

HENRY: Yup.

KIRK: Racist cops.

ALEX:	What?
KIRK:	The cops, they're racist.
HENRY:	Yes they are.

(ALEX joins GRACE.)

EFFIE:	So where were you.
KIRK:	Me.
EFFIE:	Yes you.
KIRK:	. Out.
EFFIE:	I figured that.

(EFFIE goes to the kitchen. KIRK heads for the stairs.)

HENRY:	Kirk.
KIRK:	Yo.
HENRY:	Don't run off. Sit with me for a second.

(KIRK sits next to HENRY.)

How's school.

KIRK:	Fine.
HENRY:	Good marks?

(HENRY pulls out a pen and paper.)

KIRK:	Always.
HENRY:	I want to thank you again for helping me out last weekend.
KIRK:	No problem.
HENRY:	I want you to give me the number of your parole officer. I want to tell him about the great job you did.

KIRK: No, don't do that.

HENRY: Please, I want to.

KIRK: I know you want to help, but, they...they're not impressed with...I mean...it doesn't mean anything to them. It's nice, but it doesn't help.

HENRY: Okay. Okay...you know, I need some help again this weekend.

KIRK: Oh yeah, what kind.

HENRY: Same sort of thing. Lifting boxes, a bit of painting this time. Same money as last time. You do a good job, you get a bonus, but only if you do a good job.

KIRK: Oh man. I just remembered, I got to go with a friend of mine to see his parents.

HENRY: When.

KIRK: Saturday.

HENRY: Then you can come in on Sunday.

KIRK: I was going to stay the whole weekend.

HENRY: The whole weekend?

KIRK: The whole weekend.

HENRY: Okay. I understand.

KIRK: Look man, I know you trying to hook me up and everything, but, what you do...is not my ting, you know?

HENRY: I see.

KIRK: But, you know, it's great that you trying to hook me up and everything.

HENRY: Okay.

              (KIRK gets up and starts for the stairs. GRACE, ALEX and WENDLE come in.)

GRACE: Stop right there.

KIRK: I just have to go to the washroom.

GRACE: You can go later. Effie! Come nuh!

EFFIE: *(From the kitchen offstage.)* Coming!

ALEX: Who called this meeting?

> *(EFFIE comes back in with a bowl of ice cream.)*

GRACE: That's one of the things I want to talk about. We all ready?

> *(Everyone answers.)*

Good. Now. First I want…

ALEX: Is that my ice cream.

> *(EFFIE smiles.)*

GRACE: Can I please start this now.

ALEX: Sorry.

GRACE: Okay. Now first, I want to say that I called this meeting, but maybe we should just have one every two weeks or something.

> *(No one answers.)*

It doesn't matter to me, I just want to know how you feel.

EFFIE: Well, I know for a fact that if we tell everyone to meet at a specific time and place, none of us are going to do it.

ALEX: I think if there was some money involved…

EFFIE: Don't be an ass.

WENDLE: I think the way we meet now is fine.

GRACE: Everyone agree?

(*All nod.*)

Great. Now. Rent. Here it is, the last day of the month and again I have three people who have yet to pay.

WENDLE: I paid.

GRACE: No you didn't.

WENDLE: I did. Yesterday. You forgot.

GRACE: Uh hunh.

            (*GRACE goes for her wallet and looks through it.*)

WENDLE: Henry was there.

HENRY: I'm sorry…what?

WENDLE: I pay my rent?

HENRY: Yup.

            (*She finds his cheque.*)

GRACE: Oh, okay.

EFFIE: Henry, could you toss me my purse.

GRACE: Look, I don't want to sound like a tyrant, but y'all know that the landlady is just looking for a reason to kick us out.

EFFIE: It's under the chair. There. That's it.

ALEX: You know that legally she can't do anything until the fifteenth.

            (*HENRY tosses EFFIE's purse.*)

GRACE: Look, I don't want to get angry with you, alright. Especially because you, out of all of us, have the means to pay it on time.

            (*EFFIE pulls out her cheque book and starts writing a rent cheque.*)

ALEX: So.

GRACE: So why don't you do it?

ALEX: It's not you, it's her.

GRACE: Yes, Alex, we all know the landlady is a crotchety old racist white cunt...

WENDLE: Whoa.

GRACE: We all know that she never does any repairs, we know that she thinks this is a crack house for illegal immigrants. We know. Just pay the fucking rent.

ALEX: I say if she ever fucks with us we take her to court.

             (EFFIE hands GRACE a cheque.)

WENDLE: Just pay the fucking rent and pay it on time! It's not too much to ask!

ALEX: Fine.

EFFIE: Next item?

GRACE: Oh, Kirk, you still owe for the phone bill.

KIRK: How much?

GRACE: Thirty dollars.

WENDLE/
ALEX: Ooooo.

WENDLE: You're not calling those phone sex lines or nothing are you?

ALEX: I think Junior here's got himself a girlfriend in Buffalo.

GRACE: It's none of your business guys.

WENDLE: Aren't you going to Buffalo this weekend?

KIRK: No.

ALEX: I think Junior's got himself a steady lay in Buffalo.

WENDLE: I don't think so because Junior here don't even got
                no pubic hairs man.

KIRK: Who needs pubic hairs, when I just work it boy.

                *(KIRK humps the couch. ALEX and WENDLE go
                apeshit.)*

EFFIE: Could you men please do this at another time and
                place.

GRACE: Are you finished?

                (KIRK nods.)

                Does anybody else have anything to say?

                (EFFIE and ALEX both speak at the same time.)

EFFIE: I…sorry…you go. No you go.

ALEX: I…sorry…you…no, no you go.

GRACE: Effie?

ALEX: Go.

EFFIE: It's alright.

WENDLE: One of you fucking go.

EFFIE: Okay… I don't know…who's doing this and I
                don't want to know. I don't want to make a big deal
                out of this but…someone is jerking off into a
                Kleenex and tossing it in the bin in the bathroom
                upstairs. Now, I don't care if people jerk off, but if
                you leave the Kleenex in the bin it leaves this
                smell…it's like…it's disgusting. I don't want
                to…anyway… I said what I wanted to…to say.

                (Silence.)

ALEX: It's not me, but do you really notice a smell?

EFFIE/
GRACE: Yes.

WENDLE: I've noticed it too.

                (All eyes turn to ALEX.)

ALEX: It wasn't me. *(He notices EFFIE is staring at him.)* It wasn't okay. It wasn't me!

EFFIE: I don't care. I don't want to know who it is, just stop doing it.

GRACE: Alex.

ALEX: It wasn't me!

GRACE: You wanted to say something.

ALEX: Oh. Right. Uhm… I was going to say two things: the computer needs some repairs.

WENDLE: What does that mean.

ALEX: Well. The latest version of the word processor, that I was soooo happy to get, isn't functioning properly. I'm going to take it into the shop…

GRACE: Should we all chip in some money?

ALEX: No, no I'll cover it. Until that time, constantly save your stuff on disk while you're working on it. Okay?

EFFIE: Anything else?

ALEX: Everyone, stop eating my food… I know that I, out of all of us, have the means to pay the rent on time, but I'm not a food bank. If you're really desperate, ask. That's all.

                (EFFIE lets her bowl fall on the table. She smiles.)

GRACE: Is that it?

ALEX: Yup.

GRACE:	Okay, so…
ALEX:	Oh uh…
GRACE:	What.
ALEX:	I was just fucking with you. Sorry.
EFFIE:	Oh for fuck's sake.
GRACE:	Anything else. Anybody?

(ALEX opens and closes his mouth just to piss EFFIE off.)

No? Okay. Before we all go I want to officially welcome my brother Kirk to the house.

(Everyone says "Welcome Kirk".)

And uh…it's your second week here, how do you feel…

KIRK:	It feel alright.
EFFIE:	It's good having you here.
KIRK:	Feels good to be here.
GRACE:	Okay. That's it. Kirk? Can I talk to you?

(Everyone starts to get up. GRACE pulls KIRK to the backyard.)

WENDLE:	Effie. Effie. You still want to go see *White Men Can't Jump*?
EFFIE:	Uh, well…not today.
WENDLE:	I know not today but… I've got some friends going on Saturday. I thought you might like to go…along.
EFFIE:	Uh, okay. We'll see. Okay?
WENDLE:	Right. Okay.

EFFIE: 'Cause I...

WENDLE: That's okay. Just thought I'd...I'd let you know.

EFFIE: Right.

> *(KIRK jogs out of the backyard and heads for the stairs.)*

ALEX: Yo Kirk. Come here man.

> *(KIRK stops.)*

Everything okay?

KIRK: Yeah, yeah. Hey, we going to play pool tonight?

ALEX: Not tonight. Maybe tomorrow night.

KIRK: Come on man, you gotta give me a chance to whip your ass.

ALEX: You couldn't whip my grandmother's nasty old ass motherfucka.

KIRK: Bring it on. Let's go.

> *(They play-fight a bit. KIRK wins. They say "See ya later" to each other. KIRK goes upstairs. ALEX sits on the couch. He grabs the converter.)*

HENRY: You two seem to be good friends these days.

> *(ALEX looks around for GRACE.)*

ALEX: I took him to the Bovine Sex Club last night.

HENRY: Oh yeah.

ALEX: He freaked man. The women with the leather things pushing things everywhere. He loved it.

HENRY: What is it called again?

ALEX: Bovine Sex Club? It's just a place to listen to loud music, wear dead cows, look cool. I should take you there sometime.

HENRY: Well, somehow I don't see Grace being too keen on my going to some place called the Bovine Sex Club.

ALEX: Why not.

HENRY: Oh I don't know.

            (GRACE comes back in from the backyard with some laundry. They try to look innocent. GRACE notices this. HENRY grabs the rest of the newspaper. She goes over to HENRY and hugs him. Kisses his cheek.)

GRACE: I'll be down in a second. Okay?

HENRY: Okay, okay.

            (She walks upstairs. WENDLE sits.)

ALEX: Is he going to work for you?

HENRY: Sorry?

ALEX: Is he going to work for you this weekend?

HENRY: No. No I don't think so.

ALEX: You know I'd help you, but that old Korean war wound, it's been giving me hell lately. Oh cripes, there it goes again.

HENRY: I'll be fine. I think what's most important is what you guys are doing already.

ALEX: What are we doing?

HENRY: I think that it really will help him to be with his own people.

ALEX: Oh, I see.

WENDLE: It's a really good idea but…it should be happening more often.

HENRY: I have been saying for years that what we need is a program where if you hire a young person, someone who has committed some small offence, if we put him in our businesses, you get him off the street and learning a skilled trade. That way, he will have a greater respect for himself and therefore he won't commit any crime. And in return, you give small business some tax breaks.

WENDLE: I am telling you, white people will never let it happen. They would rather see us killing each other than helping ourselves.

ALEX: Does it need to happen?

WENDLE: What?

ALEX: Is there a big problem with black youth and crime, or is it a media creation. Is it our responsibility to eliminate *all* black crime? And if we do, then what, we move on to white crime or something?

(KIRK walks down the stairs. He stops to listen to the conversation.)

HENRY: We're not trying to eliminate all black criminals.

ALEX: Then what are we talking about?

WENDLE: So, what should we do about Kirk? Should we just kick him out? Make him fend for himself?

ALEX: I think Kirk is a great guy, but he committed a crime. And be honest, if he wasn't Grace's brother, none of us would want to have anything to do with him.

WENDLE: You know Alex...we've known each other for three years now, and this is something that I've always wanted to say to you.

ALEX: Shoot.

WENDLE: With all respect, because you are a good friend, you are one of those rich niggers who doesn't believe that racism exists.

ALEX: Oh really.

WENDLE: Where I come from, you *know* it exists. You see it. You feel it. It's all around you…

ALEX: I will be the first to admit…

WENDLE: No, no, no, no, no, let me finish. Where I come from, you learn that white people are white people.

ALEX: What the hell is that supposed to mean?!

WENDLE: It means that they like to keep to themselves. They don't like strangers. They like to keep what's theirs to themselves. You know this.

ALEX: So what are you saying…

WENDLE: We have to stick together. This is the reason why I have the greatest amount of respect for the Jews, I really do, everybody swims, or everybody sinks. They help each other out, they know that together they can survive. Everybody swims or everybody sinks. It's that simple. That's why I will do anything for Kirk. Anything. We all have to stick together. This is the most racist country…

(KIRK goes to the kitchen.)

ALEX: Oh please!

WENDLE: …in the world! It's true Alex!

(GRACE walks down the stairs. She is almost ready. EFFIE pokes her head out from the top of the stairs.)

EFFIE: Could you guys keep it down, I'm trying to get some sleep.

HENRY: Are you ready to go?

GRACE: Yeah. Let's go.

(HENRY stands. Walks over to GRACE. Holds her.

KIRK walks out of the kitchen and sits on the couch. He flips through the channels.)

WENDLE: I respect you okay. You know that I respect you. But sometimes all I hear from you is that you're trying to please some invisible white man in your head.

ALEX: Oh man. The reality of what's going on in my head is by far more dangerous than that.

(GRACE and HENRY open the door and are about to leave.)

KIRK: Grace, look at that.

ALEX: What the...

(On the television they watch as a group of white youths destroy a parking lot cubicle. HENRY and GRACE are drawn to the TV.)

GRACE: What's going on?

KIRK: Look at that. Look, look... BOOM!

ALEX: Holy shit.

GRACE: Effie!

EFFIE: *(Offstage.)* What!

GRACE: You want to see this?

EFFIE: *(Offstage.)* What is it.

GRACE: I think a riot has started in Los Angeles.

EFFIE: *(Offstage.)* Oh yeah.

GRACE: You want to see this?

(EFFIE leaves her room and, wrapped in a blanket, she walks down the stairs and joins everyone in front of the TV. Something happens on the television screen to make them all jump.)

WENDLE: Where is this. Is it just outside the courthouse?

GRACE: I don't know.

ALEX: Yeah I think it is.

EFFIE: Holy shit.

        (GRACE sucks her teeth.)

ALEX: Look at that.

WENDLE: Fuck.

HENRY: My God.

        (End of ACT I.)

Act II

(Lights up on EFFIE. She lies on the couch trying to memorize terms from a textbook. KIRK walks in and goes upstairs to his room. He steps out of his room, bare-chested, onto the landing at the top of the stairs and he starts working out with a dumbbell. EFFIE doesn't notice. He starts coughing, clearing his throat to get her attention. Nothing. He takes the weight back to his room and starts to head down the stairs. He stops, sniffs his armpit, then heads back to his room. He comes out again, hops down the stairs. He goes to the kitchen. Once he's in the kitchen, EFFIE looks up from her book towards the kitchen. She gets up and creeps over to the kitchen door. KIRK is grabbing a yogurt cup from the fridge. EFFIE makes a dash for the couch. KIRK walks out of the kitchen and heads for the stairs.)

EFFIE: Kirk?

KIRK: Yo.

EFFIE: Have a couple of seconds? I need help with something.

KIRK: Sure.

EFFIE: I just have to...sit. Sit.

            (He sits at the end of the couch.)

            I just have to see how well I memorized something. Could you...

KIRK: Alright. Let's see here.

(He takes the book from her.)

EFFIE: Just read out the terms with the marks next to them. See if I get it right.

(She stretches out on the couch, absent-mindedly putting her feet on his lap.)

First one. Go for it.

KIRK: Circular reaction.

EFFIE: Circular reaction refers to a type of inter-stimulation wherein the response of one individual reproduces the stimulation that has come from another individual and in being reflected back to this individual reinforces the stimulation…well?

KIRK: I'm sorry. Yeah.

EFFIE: Yeah what?

KIRK: It's right. It's right.

EFFIE: Next.

(He surreptitiously places his hand on her knee.)

KIRK: Characteristics of social unrest.

EFFIE: A) Random behaviour. B) Excited feeling…

(He slowly moves his hand down her leg.)

EFFIE: …usually in the form of vague apprehension, aroused pugnacity…

KIRK: What's that?

EFFIE: What's what?

KIRK: Aroused pugnacity?

EFFIE: That's a good fucking question.

(She moves towards her bag to grab a dictionary, taking her leg away from him. She remembers the term before she can get her dictionary.)

It means, like a...a readiness to fight.

KIRK: Oh.

EFFIE: C) The irritability and increased suggestibility of the crowd. How am I doing there.

KIRK: Just fine. You're doing just fine.

EFFIE: Last one. Go for it.

KIRK: Okay. What is left here now? Characteristics of the acting crowd.

(She's stumped. She wriggles around trying to find the answer. She puts her foot on his thigh. It moves closer up his leg as she struggles to find the answer.)

EFFIE: I know this! I know it. Don't tell me. Don't... I know this...it's spontaneous...ah fuck. I give up. What is it. What is it.

(KIRK leans over towards her to kiss her.)

EFFIE: What.

(Just before they kiss, GRACE and ALEX enter. KIRK jumps to his feet and rushes up the stairs. GRACE walks in just in time to catch him bounding up the stairs. GRACE is carrying her knapsack, poster board and wooden sticks. ALEX is carrying two big bags of groceries and a newspaper. He goes to the kitchen.)

ALEX: I mean, if you lose nine zip to the Royals, nine points to the worst team in baseball, it means Jack Morris has got to go, is what it means.

GRACE: What's going on?

EFFIE: Nothing. Why.

(EFFIE goes to the backyard. GRACE follows.)

ALEX: What. What is it. *(No response from GRACE.)* Yo Kirk. Kirk!

KIRK: *(Offstage.)* Ya man.

ALEX: Bovine tonight!

KIRK: *(Offstage.)* I don't think so boy.

ALEX: Hey, hey, hey...what's going on here. You avoiding me or something?

            (KIRK comes out of his room.)

KIRK: No. No I'm not.

ALEX: Come on now. What's up.

KIRK: Nothing. I'm busy. That's all. Alright?

ALEX: Alright.

            (KIRK goes back to his room. EFFIE and GRACE step back inside.)

EFFIE: Alright. Fuck off.

            (Upstairs, KIRK sings. EFFIE goes upstairs.)

KIRK: "She love me now. Boy, she love me now. Ooo yeah. She love me now."

            (GRACE starts working on placards. ALEX pours himself a Scotch.)

ALEX: So what's up?

GRACE: How do you mean?

ALEX: Does Effie want to fuck Kirk or something?

GRACE: Yes she does.

ALEX: Is it really any of your business?

GRACE: He's eighteen.

ALEX: He's in his sexual prime.

GRACE: Kirk has been placed in my care.

ALEX: Is Effie going to corrupt him?

GRACE: No. That's not the point.

ALEX: Then what is the point.

GRACE: He is not here to have fun and get laid. He's here to go to school, get good grades and find a job.

ALEX: Grace, I don't know if you're aware of this but you're his sister, not his mother.

GRACE: I know I'm not his mother!

ALEX: Okay.

GRACE: I'm not doing this because I want to be his damn mother!

ALEX: Okay.

GRACE: Kirk is living here with me because he got into trouble and I take that responsibility very seriously.

ALEX: So...so your Mom...she still lives in Jamaica right?

GRACE: Yes.

ALEX: I wish my Mother lived in Jamaica. What the hell is he doing here?

GRACE: Our mother is an alcoholic. My mother's sister took me in when I was young but whenever she couldn't handle Kirk she would send him back home.

ALEX: I see.

GRACE: He has spent most of his life bouncing back and

forth. Last time he was sent back home, last Christmas, he had to pull Mummy out of some bar where some woman tried to cut her in half with a machete. She spent the night throwing up. Kirk waited up all night with her, cleaning her, making sure that she lay on her side, so that she wouldn't choke on her own vomit. When she woke up, you know what she did? She slapped him around because there was no rum in the house. That was his Christmas last year.

ALEX: That's pretty heavy.

GRACE: So I feel… I feel that he needs some stability. That's what I want for him… If…if that makes me into some kind of a mother figure… I don't think I am but…

ALEX: Do you ever go back, visit your Mom?

GRACE: No. No not at all. My mother and I…we don't get along.

ALEX: Okay.

                (GRACE shows ALEX a scar.)

GRACE: See that? That's from a kitchen knife.

KIRK: *(Offstage.)* "She love me now. Boy, she love me now. Ooo yeah. She love me now. Boy she love me now."

GRACE: Kirk needs…he needs to start thinking about a career, about school, his future. I don't want him to end up some drug dealer, beating the shit out of his girlfriend, wasting his life away. Do you understand?

ALEX: Yes I do.

GRACE: His marks are terrible. If he had a job, I'd feel better.

ALEX: I could start working on him if you like.

GRACE: Could you?

ALEX: I'll be discreet.

GRACE: And if you could kind of put it in his head that Henry is looking for someone part-time.

ALEX: Sure.

GRACE: He wants to put Kirk in the office, making good money but we can't tell him okay?

ALEX: Okay.

GRACE: Because if he knows…

KIRK: *(Offstage.)* "I gonna walk like a champion, talk like a champion…"

                (She gets ALEX to come closer.)

GRACE: Because if he knows, then…

ALEX: Then he won't work hard. I got it. Look, I'm sorry about…

                (GRACE acknowledges his apology. He tries to kiss her on the neck. She pulls away frantically.)

GRACE: You're not going to make a pass at him either, are you.

ALEX: No.

GRACE: Have you told him about…

ALEX: My sexual proclivity? No. He's a bit too straight. Know what I mean. You have to be careful. But who knows. Maybe he's checking me out.

                (GRACE laughs.)

        And he sure does have a mighty fine ass…

GRACE: Alex.

ALEX: It was a joke. I was just kidding.

                 (*KIRK jumps down the stairs. Fully clothed. He
                 heads towards the kitchen. GRACE nudges ALEX.*)

                 Yo Kirk. Come on over here!

                 (*KIRK goes over to ALEX.*)

KIRK: What's up.

ALEX: Look, I want you to tell me the truth and I don't
                 want you to lie to me okay! You lie to me, I'll kill
                 you, you understand me!

KIRK: Okay, okay! What's up man!

ALEX: Was that you singing upstairs or was that the radio
                 or something?

KIRK: You really think it was the radio?

ALEX: No, I'm just fucking with you. But it sounded good
                 though.

KIRK: Thanks.

ALEX: So pull some out. Let's see it.

KIRK: No, no.

ALEX: Come on. You got to give your sister over here a
                 taste. You got to.

KIRK: No.

ALEX: Here look...I know you must be a little nervous.
                 Tell you what, I'll do the drum machine part.
                 Okay? Join in any time. You ready? Here we go.
                 One, two, one two three four...

                 (*ALEX demonstrates that he has no rhythm. KIRK
                 and GRACE laugh.*)

ALEX: Come on man. Quick, join in. Whicky, whicky,
                 whicky.

GRACE:	Alex… Al… *Alex!* There's a white man inside you just dying to get out.
ALEX:	Har de har har.
GRACE:	Go ahead. I'd like to hear it.

(KIRK gets up and pulls a tape out of his pocket.)

KIRK:	Alright, alright. I just so happen to have a tape here.

(He puts the tape into the stereo. Music starts.)

KIRK:	This selection is goin' out to all de stations in Toronto. It goin' out to 102.5, 106.9 and what's you favourite station?
GRACE:	I don't have one.
KIRK:	88.1! Here we go now. "There was a girl. And she make me want to…wind my body down so low. She make me want to…"

(KIRK notices that EFFIE is sitting and listening at the top of the stairs.)

That's all ya gettin fa now.

(ALEX and GRACE applaud.)

GRACE:	It good still Kirk.
ALEX:	That was *great!*
KIRK:	Thanks.
ALEX:	So, you have a stage name or something?
KIRK:	Ya man. Captain Kirk. You know, like *Star Trek.*
ALEX:	Right right.
KIRK:	The first CD, check it. "Enterprise".
ALEX:	You know what?

KIRK: What.

ALEX: I don't know if you're aware of this, but I've got another computer in my room, it has a slot for a soundcard...

KIRK: Uh hunh.

ALEX: Now a sound card...think of it as a...a mini recording studio.

(EFFIE goes back into her room.)

KIRK: Right, right.

ALEX: If you want to get one, I can install it for you and then bingo, there you go man. Your own instant recording studio. You can record whatever you want, whenever you want. Four tracks, CD quality sound...

KIRK: That would be a bonus you know. 'Cause as it stand right now, I have to truck my equipment all the way across town just to get to my friend's studio.

ALEX: Well?

KIRK: And how much do these sound cards cost.

ALEX: Around four hundred bucks. But what you can do is, you can give Henry a call, tell him you want to earn four hundred bucks real fast and bingo...sound card's yours.

KIRK: I see. Alright. Alright.

ALEX: And if you get it, and I install it for you...you can *keep* the computer 'cause I never use it.

KIRK: No, I couldn't do that.

ALEX: Hey, look at me. Hey look, look right at me, don't worry about it.

KIRK: I see. I see. Alright.

ALEX: The offer's there. Think about it. All I want from you is when you accept your little Grammy award, I want you to look in the camera and I want you to thank me.

KIRK: Alright, we'll do, we'll do.

             (ALEX starts to go upstairs. EFFIE comes downstairs. He stops in his tracks, turns and goes to the backyard, grabbing his newspaper as he goes. KIRK eats the yogurt that he started eating before. EFFIE looks for a newspaper. KIRK stares at her. GRACE stares at him.)

GRACE: Is that all you eat now?

KIRK: Sorry?

GRACE: Is yogurt all you eat now?

KIRK: No.

GRACE: You eating properly?

KIRK: Yeah.

GRACE: I don't see you buying food with the money I give you.

KIRK: Alright, alright.

EFFIE: Did you get today's paper?

             (KIRK stares at EFFIE. GRACE grabs her paper from her bag, smacks KIRK on the head with it, hands her newspaper over to EFFIE. EFFIE looks at the front page.)

             Holy fuck.

GRACE: What?

EFFIE: When did this happen?

GRACE: What?

EFFIE: Some white guy got beaten up.

GRACE: Yeah, I saw that.

EFFIE: Pulled out of his car and…

GRACE: Yeah.

EFFIE: Oh this is great.

                    (EFFIE grabs her textbook and notebook.)

GRACE: What?

EFFIE: Everything is dovetailing so perfectly for my course.

GRACE: Oh yeah.

EFFIE: You've got to hear this.

GRACE: What.

EFFIE: "Characteristics of the Acting Crowd: Instead of acting on the basis of established rule, it acts on the basis of aroused impulse. It is not strange that much of the crowd's behaviour should be violent, cruel and destructive because impulses that would ordinarily be subject to a severe check by the individual's judgment, now has a free passage to expression."

GRACE: Hmm.

EFFIE: ʾ   That's what's happening right now. This guy that was pulled out of his truck. That's what's happened to him.

GRACE: You want to help me with these slogans? I need like four slogans.

                    (EFFIE grabs some poster board and a large magic marker.)

EFFIE: Isn't it wild though that we're like living through this really tumultuous time. Doesn't it like…

GRACE: No.

            (WENDLE walks in the front door. He has his textbooks. ALEX enters, pours himself a Scotch, and sits at the computer.)

EFFIE: Is it "No Peace No Justice" or is it "No Justice No Peace".

GRACE: I think it's "No Justice No Peace".

            (EFFIE starts writing.)

            Do you think there's going to be violence?

EFFIE: Where?

GRACE: At the rally?

EFFIE: Probably yeah.

GRACE: You think so?

EFFIE: All the symptoms are there. General restlessness, feeling of unease…aroused pugnacity.

            (KIRK laughs.)

ALEX: There isn't going to be any violence.

EFFIE: You don't think so?

ALEX: This is Canada for crying out loud.

WENDLE: Nova Scotia has had a long history of racial strife my friend.

GRACE: There were riots here back in 1933. A group of Jewish people were playing softball when they were attacked by some jocks from an upper-class yacht club. The Christie Pits riot.

EFFIE: In Montreal they riot over hockey.

GRACE: Are you going to the rally?

ALEX: I was thinking about it but the organizers are trying to make this recent police shooting on the weekend into some kind of Canadian Rodney King…

WENDLE: Tell me something, why do you hate black people so much?

ALEX: I don't hate black people, I just have a hard time equating the shooting of a knife-wielding drug dealer in Toronto with the beating of Rodney King!

WENDLE: Aww get the fuck out of my face right now…

ALEX: Wendle! I know the kid was a black youth and that we all have to sink or swim, but he was a drug dealer!

WENDLE: *(Yelling.)* He was holding a knife!

ALEX: *(Yelling.)* What do you expect a police officer to do!

WENDLE: *(Yelling.)* Why the fuck do you have to shoot someone holding a knife!

ALEX: *(Yelling.)* A knife is still a deadly weapon Wendle!

WENDLE: Oh just fucking go back to those white people…you love white people so much just fucking go back to them. If you didn't hang around those people you wouldn't be the way you are!

ALEX: What did you just say?

WENDLE: Nothing.

ALEX: What the fuck was that supposed to mean.

WENDLE: You know I didn't say what I said. Alex, you know I didn't mean…

                (ALEX exits.)

                (Shouting.) Oh fuck off Alex! You know I didn't

mean what you thought I meant. Alex... Alex. Fuck you man. Fuck you.

(WENDLE grabs his books. He turns to EFFIE.)

I didn't mean it the way it came out.

GRACE: I need a slogan.

EFFIE: Yeah.

(WENDLE sees he is being ignored. Goes upstairs.)

GRACE: I can only take so much of that man.

EFFIE: He reminds me of my father. It really pisses me off.

GRACE: Okay. Think think think think...slogan.

EFFIE: Can I turn on some music?

GRACE: No. God I don't want to hear no more o dat damn Trini music in this house...

EFFIE: What's wrong with Trini music?

(GRACE stands and moves her hips.)

GRACE: "Cent, Five Cent, Ten Cent... Loonie."

EFFIE: Sit.

GRACE: It's not my fault Trinidadians can't write good music. Why should I have to suffer to listen to it.

(EFFIE hits her with the newspaper.)

That hurt!

EFFIE: Good.

(GRACE points to the cardboard and marker.)

GRACE: Get to work!

EFFIE: Do you think things are going to change now that Bob Rae's in office?

GRACE: Yeah, well I hope so. I don't know…

EFFIE: Wasn't he there at the rally?

GRACE: Oh don't get me started.

EFFIE: Started on what?

GRACE: It was a rally organized by the black community because there has been another shooting of a black youth here in Toronto by the police. Bob Rae showed up because he has always shown up even before he was Premier. I don't see Nobody from the Liberal party, Nobody from the Conservative party. He opens his mouth, not two seconds later, you have these white men screaming, "Hey Bob, what's the story, why you acting like a Tory."

EFFIE: Really.

GRACE: You have a bunch of white men from the so-called labour movement shouting down the only provincial leader that has promised to strengthen employment equity—

EFFIE: Did…

GRACE: —and the white men on Bay street are paying for big billboards ridiculing him, and they don't give a damn that a young black man is dead. Let the man do his work before we tear him to pieces.

EFFIE: Why don't you write "I love you Bob."

GRACE: Alright, alright.

EFFIE: Seriously. In big block letters "Bob, do me."

GRACE: Alright already.

EFFIE: You'd fuck Bob Rae wouldn't you.

GRACE: I think he's cute. I don't know if I'd go all the way but yeah, I think he's cute.

EFFIE: Get the fuck out of here.

GRACE: What?

EFFIE: Get the fuck out of here.

GRACE: What.

EFFIE: You need serious help.

GRACE: As if you should talk, going after my 18 year-old brother.

EFFIE: So.

GRACE: So you're the freak.

EFFIE: Well you better tell him to stop walking around without a shirt on. I swear to God one day...

GRACE: Effie...

EFFIE: I know I know, he's not here to get laid, I know. It's just...after Alex fucking jumped out of the fucking closet, I need... You don't want to know what I need. So Bob Rae: do you think he's...

            (*She motions with her hands to imply he has a large penis.*)

GRACE: Huge. You know the CN Tower? Bigger.

EFFIE: Do you think he's bigger than Henry?

            (*GRACE says nothing.*)

            No.

GRACE: Effie.

EFFIE: Henry has a small... NO.

GRACE: Don't you dare tell anybody!

EFFIE: Awww, honey.

GRACE: Well it's not like...it's kinda...well...

(GRACE tries to show EFFIE exactly how small it is.)

EFFIE: But is it like…

GRACE: No, it's still pretty thick.

EFFIE: But he's got such a deep voice.

GRACE: Effie, you can't tell anybody. I'm serious. Don't.

EFFIE: Sure okay. Don't worry. You must really love him.

(There is a knock at the door.)

Who is it?

HENRY: *(Offstage.)* Is anybody home?

EFFIE: Come on in, Mr. Stubbs.

(GRACE slaps EFFIE. HENRY opens the door and steps in. He is carrying a tool case. GRACE runs over and hugs him.)

HENRY: Sorry?

GRACE: Hello honey!

(She kisses him.)

HENRY: What did I do wrong?

GRACE: Nothing…

HENRY: Hi Effie.

EFFIE: Hellooo.

HENRY: Could you help me with…I still have some tools to get out of the truck.

GRACE: Sure. Sure thing.

(HENRY leaves. GRACE points at EFFIE on her way out. EFFIE grabs a paper towel roll and holds

it to her groin. KIRK bounds down the stairs. EFFIE
hides in the kitchen. He is carrying a knapsack and
talking on the cordless phone.)

KIRK: I coming just now. You follow me? A'ight Junior.

(He returns the phone to the base and pulls a Post-it
note off it. He knits his brow and crumples it up. He
thinks for a second and then opens the knapsack.
EFFIE sneaks up behind him and jumps on his
back.)

EFFIE: Where do you think you're going?

KIRK: Hey…

(He carries her around the couch.)

EFFIE: You think you can just waltz out of here without
telling me where you are going to and when you'll
be back?! You've got another thing coming buster!

KIRK: I can do whatever I want.

EFFIE: Oh you think so do you.

KIRK: Get off me.

EFFIE: No.

KIRK: Get off me.

EFFIE: Make me.

KIRK: Get off!

(He tosses her on the couch.)

EFFIE: I can't believe you just did that!

KIRK: Oh yeah.

EFFIE: Help me up.

(He takes her hand and helps her up. She hits him
really hard in the abdomen. He is winded a bit.)

Are you okay. I didn't mean to hit you that hard. Honestly. Are you okay?

KIRK: You wanna box with Kirk eh?

             (He circles the couch, she follows him.)

EFFIE: I wouldn't want to hurt you.

KIRK: You can't hurt me.

EFFIE: Don't make me hurt you.

KIRK: Come on. Let's go.

EFFIE: I'm warning you.

             (EFFIE takes a jujitsu stance.)

Don't make me hurt you. Take your best shot. Go ahead.

             (KIRK tags her shoulder with an open hand.)

Oh that really hurt. Have you met my side kick?

             (EFFIE makes a well placed martial arts kick to his thigh. He tries the same. She grabs his leg and strikes out with her fist, stopping ever so near his groin.)

I could have got you! I didn't, but I could have. Are you scared?

KIRK: A little.

             (KIRK does a Bruce Lee battle cry and tries to dazzle her with improvised kung fu moves. EFFIE laughs, grabs one of his arms and holds him close. She kisses him. She shoves him on to the couch. He grabs her and they kiss. A truck door closes outside. EFFIE pulls away. KIRK tries to continue, EFFIE shoves him away. We can hear GRACE and HENRY talking outside.)

GRACE: *(Offstage.)* So I couldn't go to that class.

HENRY: *(Offstage.)* Oh yeah.

EFFIE: Go. *Go.* Get going. Quick.

KIRK: No don't do that.

> *(EFFIE grabs his knapsack. As she picks it up, the contents fall out: a video cassette, a Walkman, and a gun. They both see it. KIRK grabs everything and stuffs it back in his knapsack. The door opens. EFFIE and KIRK look at each other. GRACE and HENRY walk in carrying boxes of tools.)*

GRACE: Then, I was late for my aerobics so I didn't go to that either...

HENRY: Didn't you read that book I gave you about prioritizing?

GRACE: No, not yet.

> *(KIRK leaves, pushing past them.)*

What's going on?

EFFIE: Nothing.

GRACE: What did you just do.

EFFIE: Nothing.

> *(EFFIE goes to the backyard. GRACE knits her brow and shakes her head.)*

HENRY: If you want things to happen you are going to have to prioritize.

GRACE: Look, I know I'm not the most prompt person in the world.

HENRY: Why don't you drop your aerobics class, I mean, I like you big anyway.... I mean I like you the way you are... I mean...could you pass me that box?

(She does. EFFIE walks back in and sits on the couch.)

EFFIE: Guys.

         (They both look at EFFIE.)

I have to talk to you.

HENRY: Are you okay?

EFFIE: Grace.

         (EFFIE motions for them to sit on the couch. They do.)

Kirk has a gun.

GRACE: WHAT?!

EFFIE: We were goofing around and I saw it in his knapsack.

         (ALEX bursts in the room with a bunch of videos.)

ALEX: Is the sound fixed yet?

HENRY: No not yet.

EFFIE: Alex come here.

ALEX: What. What's wrong? What?

GRACE: Effie found a gun in Kirk's knapsack.

EFFIE: We were play-fighting and I saw it.

ALEX: Fuck.

GRACE: *(In a Jamaican accent.)* Stupid. Stupid. Fucking idiot.

ALEX: What are we going to do?

EFFIE: I think we should call a house meeting right now.

GRACE: Good idea. Is Wendle here.

EFFIE: He's upstairs. I think he's taking a nap.

(GRACE jumps up and goes upstairs.)

ALEX: Henry, is the sound fixed yet?

HENRY: No, not yet. I may have it fixed by tonight, don't hold your breath.

EFFIE: Why? What'd you get?

(WENDLE walks down the stairs with GRACE. ALEX does his best Marlon Brando.)

ALEX: *On the Waterfront* and *Guys and Dolls*. It's a Marlon Brando extravaganza this evening ladies and gentlemen...

WENDLE: So what's going on.

EFFIE: I was goofing around with Kirk and I found a gun in his knapsack.

(Pause.)

ALEX: Well I think we should talk to him. Find out what's going on...

WENDLE: I want him out of this house and that's it.

(WENDLE stands up to leave.)

ALEX: Now hold on a second...

WENDLE: Don't hold on a second me! I don't want to have to worry about some niggers driving by and plugging my body full of holes! I had enough trouble with fucking white kids beating the shit out of me all through high school, I don't need to worry about some fucking dumb nigger with a fucking Uzi ripping apart my fucking living room!

ALEX: I don't think what's needed here is a lot of anger.

WENDLE: I'm not angry. No. I'm hurt. I welcomed him into my home. I treated him like a brother. No. Send the fucking nigger back to Jamaica.

GRACE: What the hell is that supposed to mean?

WENDLE: You heard me. If he doesn't want to live and abide by the laws of my country, send the fucking nigger back to Jamaica.

GRACE: *(Yelling.)* What the hell do you mean your country. I'm Jamaican and this is just as much my country as it is yours.

WENDLE: The hell you mean you're Jamaican. You were raised in Montreal since you were three! I don't give a fuck where you were born. I don't give a fuck about that little accent you pull out every now and then, you as Jamaican as fucking Henry.

HENRY: What about all the things you said about swimming together. I mean Kirk is a stranger to this country. He is an immigrant like me and…

WENDLE: You ever pick up a gun?

HENRY: No, but I mean, it's not easy being an immigrant in this country, especially if you're black they don't respect your education, your training…

WENDLE: Have you ever picked up a gun?

HENRY: No but surely we have to try harder to reach out to him…

WENDLE: *(Yelling.)* Have you ever fucking picked up a motherfucking gun?!

HENRY: *(Just as loudly.)* No.

WENDLE: No. No you haven't. And I know it's going to be hard for you to hear me say this, but it's the way I feel. I am sick and tired of these fucking Jamaicans coming into this country and doing crack and shooting each other and shit!

          (GRACE knocks over a chair and goes into the backyard.)

ALEX: Wendle!

WENDLE: I'm sick of it. Every news report, you don't see any
               Somalis shooting each other do ya. Why? 'Cause
               they are grateful to be in this country, as they damn
               well should be.

               (HENRY leaves.)

EFFIE: You're such a fucking asshole.

WENDLE: I'm not going to lie about the way I feel.

ALEX: So what do you think we should do.

EFFIE: I think you had a good idea. I'll see if I can talk to
               Kirk. Find out what's going on.

ALEX: Meeting adjourned?

EFFIE: Yeah, I'll tell Grace.

WENDLE: You understand where I'm coming from right?

EFFIE: It's okay Wendle.

WENDLE: I mean, I can't be untrue to what I feel.

EFFIE: I know.

WENDLE: You're not mad at me are you?

EFFIE: Why would I be mad at you Wendle.

WENDLE: If anybody calls, I'm taking a nap.

EFFIE: Okay.

               *(WENDLE gets up and goes upstairs. EFFIE
               realizes that she is alone with ALEX. She heads for
               the stairs.)*

ALEX: Can we call a truce for five minutes.

EFFIE: Sure.

ALEX: Grace wants you to slow down with Kirk.

EFFIE: If Grace has anything she wants to say to me, she can say it to my face.

ALEX: I think you should slow down with Kirk.

EFFIE: It's none of your fucking business.

ALEX: I don't think that was five minutes.

EFFIE: Guess not.

ALEX: I want to stop this antagonism. I find it incredibly childish.

EFFIE: You lied to me. You put my life at risk…

ALEX: I didn't put your life at risk!

(EFFIE and ALEX speak simultaneously.)

EFFIE: You could have infected me with… How do you expect me to… How do I know that! How do I know that!

ALEX: Oh for fuck's sake, everything that I did with him was absolutely safe, I made sure that everything we did was absolutely safe. I would never…

(Silence.)

Being gay doesn't mean you have AIDS.

EFFIE: I don't want to talk about this with you anymore. I get sick. I find it… I find it disgusting. It makes me ill.

ALEX: When are you moving out?

EFFIE: Not soon enough.

ALEX: I don't want you to move out. I'm sorry about what happened and the way you found out. I am. I am very, *very* sorry. But can't we…our friendship meant so much to me and…is there some….

EFFIE: No.

(EFFIE goes upstairs. ALEX sits on the couch. KIRK walks in the front door without his knapsack.)

KIRK: Alex?

(GRACE and HENRY enter the living room. She sees KIRK.)

GRACE: You. Come here.

ALEX: Uh, Grace, maybe you should talk to Effie first.

GRACE: Why the hell would I want to talk to Effie? You. Come. Now.

(He walks towards her.)

Move your ass. Move it!

(GRACE shoves him outside. ALEX pours himself a stiff drink.)

(Offstage.) What the hell you mean you don't know...because you've embarrassed me, you embarrass me in front of me friends.

HENRY: Are you going to the rally?

ALEX: I don't know. Are you?

HENRY: Unless I can find a really good excuse.

GRACE: *(Offstage.)* Listen now Kirk, I don't want to hear anymore of ya nonsense! Lord give me the pillow and take the case!

HENRY: How are you doing? Are you okay?

ALEX: Yeah I'm fine. Do you mind if I turn the TV around?

HENRY: No. Go ahead.

(ALEX turns the TV around. Turns it on.)

ALEX: Anything in particular you want to watch?

HENRY: No, no. I've been thinking about filing a complaint with the police.

ALEX: And...

HENRY: ...If I went, would you go with me?

ALEX: Sure. Of course.

HENRY: Because I... I would like you to go with me.

ALEX: Sure.

HENRY: You're from Ottawa right?

ALEX: Yup. Born and raised.

HENRY: Did you have to deal with a lot of racism when you were growing up?

ALEX: Not really. No. I had some kids make fun of my hair in grade school, but that's just...kids being kids.

HENRY: What about your parents?

ALEX: I don't know. I don't think so. If they did, they never told me. Then again, I spent a lot of time in boarding school so...why do you ask?

HENRY: Just curious.

ALEX: Oh.

     (Short pause.)

HENRY: Sometimes I think that after 300 years of revolt and riots and discussion and reconstruction and Martin Luther King and Rosa Parks and Marcus Garvey and Mandela and all the others, we... I wish we could just stop and make our own way and not have to struggle all the time to prove that we are equal. And when I see a black person has committed a crime in the newspaper, I don't feel that he is jeopardizing 300 years of hard work. And if that one person commits a crime, it's because he's human, and sometimes, that's what human beings do. Know what I mean?

ALEX: Yes.

(KIRK and GRACE come back inside.)

GRACE: Kirk has something he wants to say.

KIRK: I just want to say how sorry I am. I know that you all care for me and if you give me one more chance, I know I won't let you down.

HENRY: Okay.

ALEX: Okay.

GRACE: I'm going to get Wendle and Effie. You stay here.

(GRACE goes upstairs. Once she is out of earshot…)

ALEX: She took a chunk out of you didn't she.

KIRK: Booooy ya don't know.

ALEX: Don't mess with Jamaican women man.

KIRK: I know it. I know it.

ALEX: So…you know you fucked up right?

KIRK: Yes sir.

ALEX: Don't call me sir.

HENRY: Was it your gun or what's going on…

KIRK: No, no, see…I got this friend, he's not really a friend…I just know him right? He give me this bag to hold for him. I don't know what's in it and I don't want to know. But upstairs, I get kinda curious. I look in it, I see the gun, boom. I call him up right away, ya following me? I tell him, "Junior, I don't want this thing here in my possession." And as I'm taking it to him, Effie find it in the bag. I don't blame her for being shocked right? 'Cause I was shock just the same way. But I am telling you…I have nothing to do with that gun, you understand. You understand?

ALEX: Yeah I understand, I just don't think you should hang out with this guy anymore.

KIRK: True, true.

ALEX: You want to go out, you want to go for beer or play pool, give me a shout, alright?

KIRK: Cool.

(*ALEX shakes KIRK's hand. KIRK puts his arm around ALEX in a semi-hug.*)

ALEX: It's alright.

KIRK: And Henry, I really appreciate what all you done for me.

(*He shakes HENRY's hand.*)

HENRY: I still need some help, if you…

GRACE: (*Offstage.*) Kirk, could you come up here please.

KIRK: I'll be back.

(*KIRK rushes upstairs.*)

ALEX: So what do you think.

HENRY: What do you think?

ALEX: I don't know. I…I don't know.

(*ALEX rushes to the television.*)

HENRY: Well, we all have to stick together.

ALEX: Yeah. Yeah.

(*Blackout.*

End of ACT II.)

Act III

(Lights up. WENDLE sits studying at the dining table with a calculator and notebook. HENRY has pulled apart the television and is putting it back together.)

WENDLE: So how are the repairs coming. Henry? Henry. Henry.

HENRY: Yes.

WENDLE: How are the repairs.

HENRY: Fine.

WENDLE: Need a hand? Henry.

HENRY: What?

WENDLE: Need a hand?

HENRY: No.

WENDLE: Alright.

(GRACE walks in the front door.)

How was the protest, Grace? Grace?

GRACE: Hmm?

WENDLE: How was the protest.

GRACE: Great.

WENDLE: Was there any violence?

GRACE: No.

WENDLE: Well that's good.

          (GRACE starts walking up the stairs. She stops.)

GRACE: Don't talk to me like there is nothing going on. I
              hate that.

WENDLE: Alright.

GRACE: My aunt and uncle are from Jamaica. They worked
              their fingers to the bone trying to make it in this
              country. My aunt worked as a maid and my uncle
              worked as a trolley-car porter because in Montreal
              in those days, those were the jobs they gave to
              black people. They saved every penny they had to
              give me the education they felt I deserved. And
              they are not alone. All over this country there are
              Jamaicans just like them, and even though I was
              raised in Montreal, I was born in Jamaica and I am
              proud to call it my place of birth just as I am proud
              of the people who come from it.

                  (She walks towards the stairs.)

WENDLE: Grace. Don't go. Listen, when I get angry I say
              stupid things.

GRACE: I know.

WENDLE: I guess I've been reading the *Toronto Sun* too much.

GRACE: Don't read the *Sun*.

WENDLE: I read it for the sports page.

GRACE: You know the Heritage Front says that most of the
              things you hear on its phone line you can read in
              an editorial of the *Toronto Sun*.

WENDLE: So? The fuck do I care, they have a great sports
              page.

GRACE: Have mercy.

(GRACE goes upstairs. EFFIE and ALEX burst in the door. ALEX has a bloody piece of cloth and is pinching the bridge of his nose.)

EFFIE: Help somebody! Quick!

ALEX: I'm alright. Really.

WENDLE: What the fuck!

HENRY: Grace!

(HENRY and WENDLE run to help EFFIE and ALEX.)

ALEX: It just looks bad, that's all.

HENRY: I'll get some ice. Grace!

ALEX: No, no, no, no. I think it's dried. See?

(He stops pinching. GRACE enters.)

HENRY: Come to the sink and get cleaned up.

ALEX: I don't need to be cleaned up.

EFFIE: Wendle, go to the kitchen, fill a bowl with warm water and grab a clean towel.

GRACE: I'll get the towel.

(WENDLE and GRACE leave.)

HENRY: How did this happen?

ALEX: Someone started a fight. I stuck my nose in there, got a little love tap. I'm fine.

HENRY: People are fighting each other?

EFFIE: Henry…there's a riot on Yonge Street.

ALEX: I don't know if I would call it a riot. It is definitely a melee.

HENRY: Where's Kirk?

(EFFIE and ALEX look at each other.)

ALEX: Well, I thought he was…

EFFIE: We don't know where he is.

> *(GRACE and WENDLE return with towel and bowl. ALEX cleans himself.)*

WENDLE: So what happened man, are you okay?

HENRY: There's a riot on Yonge street.

GRACE: Where's Kirk?

HENRY: Let's go look for him.

> *(HENRY and GRACE jump up and get ready to leave.)*

EFFIE: Let me just get my camera.

> *(EFFIE grabs her camera from the bookshelf.)*

GRACE: Where did you see him last?

> *(They head out talking. WENDLE closes the door.)*

ALEX: Man.

WENDLE: So what happened?

ALEX: Uh, there was the protest in front of the U.S. embassy. There were some Nazi skinheads across the street shouting stuff. Then a black woman leaves the crowd, runs across the street and does a flying leap kick at the biggest Nazi skinhead of them all. He falls, they all just scatter, like that.

WENDLE: Major props to our beautiful black sisters.

ALEX: Hear, hear.

WENDLE: So that's when the fighting started?

ALEX: No, no, no. So we got up to Queen's Park. People

started to sit in the middle of the intersections. And then the cops came. Some people got really roughed up. We headed down...let's see, I think that's when we got split up. I went down Bay Street. And then someone threw a rock through a window...

WENDLE: That's when it started?

ALEX: Well, kinda. It's like...it was sort of scary, but it was still kind of Canadian, you know...it's like, there was violence, but it was still kinda polite violence. I don't know.

WENDLE: Were there a lot of black people?

ALEX: Well...the crowd was mixed... I don't know...

WENDLE: How'd you get the nose?

ALEX: Then I crossed over to Church Street. I just caught a glimpse of what was happening on Yonge and it looked a lot more violent. A lot of young kids, angry, smashing store windows and just grabbing stuff. I just got a glimpse of what was happening. I'm passing through this parking lot on Church and this Global TV camera man is standing there, black guy starts shoving him around. I pull him off and he cold cocks me.

WENDLE: Oh.

ALEX: I couldn't believe it. Some motherfucker starts going, "You oppressive white bastard." Right? But who does he hit, he hits me. You've got to go out there. It's wild out there.

WENDLE: No it's okay.

ALEX: No I mean it man, you should be out there.

WENDLE: It wouldn't be a good idea for me to go out there right now.

ALEX: Hey I understand. You're being responsible. That's good. Well I'm going back out there!

WENDLE: Alex. Be careful.

            (ALEX leaves. KIRK runs in through the back door. He is carrying a brand new video camera in his hand. He is out of breath. He drops the video camera on the couch and catches his breath.)

WENDLE: Don't you move. Everyone is looking for you.

KIRK: Wendle.

WENDLE: What's that you got there?

KIRK: Someone smash a window on some store on Yonge Street. Then a whole crowd just start passing the stuff out...

WENDLE: No, no, no, no, no, no...

KIRK: I didn't steal it, I swear! I swear I didn't steal it! I'm not in for stealing or nothing, but when it is put in you hand you know you can't refuse.

WENDLE: Tomorrow morning you are going to take that back. Stay right here till Grace gets back.

KIRK: But...

WENDLE: No. No, no, no, no. Fuck you. No buts.

KIRK: But...

WENDLE: You have any idea who you're talking to? You are talking to a man who is going to own a store like that one day. You're looking at a man who is going to own a whole chain of stores just like that. You're taking it back tomorrow.

KIRK: Yes sir.

WENDLE: You understand me?

KIRK: Yes sir.

                 (KIRK is about to step out the front door.)

WENDLE: HEY!

                 (KIRK stops.)

WENDLE: You stay right there and don't move till Grace gets
                 back.

                 *(KIRK sits, one hand on his crotch. WENDLE
                 shakes his head and goes to his room. EFFIE walks
                 in the front door.)*

EFFIE: Are you okay?

                 *(EFFIE puts her camera on the table. While her back
                 is turned, he shoves the video camera under a
                 cushion of the couch.)*

                 What, you're not talking to me? Hey.

                 (She touches his head. He sharply pulls away.)

                 You know what? I'll tell you a secret. And this is a…
                 I used to be a really fat and ugly kid. It's true. And
                 uh…I grew up in Vancouver…it was just my Mom
                 and me and in the early 80s she lost her job, so we
                 had no money. She had a nervous breakdown, I
                 have to take care of her, I'm fat, ugly, and…I went
                 through a thing that…that was so painful. And I
                 wanted so much to…for someone to reach out and
                 put their hand on my shoulder and reach out to me,
                 but I didn't trust anyone. I couldn't because if I let
                 someone touch me they could hurt me too. People
                 tried to reach out to me and I lashed out at them.
                 And then I wanted to destroy myself. I became
                 very self-destructive. I just wanted… I wanted
                 someone to…

                 (EFFIE slowly places her hand on his shoulder.)

                 Shhh.

(These next two lines overlap.)

KIRK: But you don't know, you don't know…

EFFIE: Yes I do. Yes I do.

> *(WENDLE walks down the stairs with a textbook and calculator in hand. He stops when he sees them in an embrace. He continues down the stairs. KIRK and EFFIE pull apart. WENDLE walks to the table. Stands there.)*

WENDLE: So, things are crazy out there.

KIRK: Yeah man.

WENDLE: You didn't do any fighting did you.

KIRK: Some faggot try to rough me up but I…

WENDLE: Watch the language.

KIRK: Yes sir.

> *(WENDLE stops working and looks up from his books at KIRK.)*

WENDLE: Don't use the word faggot around Alex.

KIRK: Why.

WENDLE: 'Cause he's gay.

KIRK: WHAT!

WENDLE: He's gay.

KIRK: You joking.

WENDLE: No. No I'm not.

> *(KIRK looks at EFFIE.)*

KIRK: Alex a faggot?

WENDLE: Just thought I'd let you know.

(GRACE, HENRY and ALEX return. GRACE rushes over to KIRK.)

GRACE: Are you okay? I was worried there for a moment.

KIRK: I'm fine.

ALEX: That's what I told them.

KIRK: I'm fine.

EFFIE: Alex is a hero, he saved a white man.

ALEX: Oh it was nothing, really.

(WENDLE walks over to the couch. He looks for the video camera.)

WENDLE: Where is it?

GRACE: What...

(WENDLE rifles through the cushions, finds the video camera. Hands it to GRACE.)

What is this?

KIRK: I can explain.

WENDLE: He's taking it back tomorrow morning.

GRACE: What the hell is this?

KIRK: I can explain. I was walking through the crowd, somebody walk up to me and shove it in my hand, I swear I didn't steal it. Don't look at me like that! I'm telling you the truth! You're just like Auntie June, you never believe me! I am...

GRACE: Shut up.

KIRK: I swear, I swear, I swear...

GRACE: Shut up!

EFFIE: I think...

GRACE: Shhhh!

            *(She puts the video camera down. She takes a finger
            and pokes KIRK's head.)*

KIRK: Don't do that.

GRACE: You don't like that?

            (She does it again.)

KIRK: I telling you, don't do that.

GRACE: I am supposed to be looking out for you…

KIRK: I…

GRACE: Shut up! I don't know what to say to you anymore.
            Are you stupid?! Are you insane?! All these people
            working hard, for you. Do you not care?

ALEX: Grace…

GRACE: Shut the fuck up… You are on probation for one
            crime and you commit another. What are we
            supposed to do for you now. Are we supposed to
            lie to your probation officer when he finds out that
            you were looting, do you want us to lie? Is that
            what you want!? Let me ask you something Kirk,
            do you think that I had all of this? Hmm? Do you
            think I had all this?

            (She shoves him.)

ALEX: Grace…

GRACE: Do you think I had people caring for me willing to
            give me chance after chance after chance!

            *(She starts slapping him around. She unintention-
            ally shoves him towards ALEX. ALEX tries to pull
            KIRK away from her.)*

KIRK: Don't touch me!

EFFIE: Grace!

ALEX: Come on, Grace!

           (*She continues to shove him. ALEX touches KIRK's shoulder.*)

KIRK: Don't touch me!

           (*ALEX tries to step in between KIRK and GRACE. He holds KIRK's shoulders, in the process. KIRK shoves ALEX down violently.*)

           Just get your faggoty hands off me. Fucking faggot. Right.

           (*He pulls out a gun. He fires it twice in the air.*)

           Y'all pretend but ya don't give a damn about me. What, you think I don't know? You think I don't know shame? Eh?

           (*He places the gun to ALEX's back.*)

           Hear me? You think I don't know shame? I gonna ask you one more time, you think I don't know shame?

ALEX: Yes you know shame.

           (*He backs away and spits on ALEX.*)

KIRK: Check it. I gone.

           (*He exits. Silence.*)

WENDLE: Well, if the landlady had any doubts that this was a crack house, the two bullets in the ceiling will definitely help.

           (*EFFIE goes to the phone. HENRY goes to GRACE and hugs her.*)

HENRY: You okay?

WENDLE: We should all go. The police are going to be here. Alex.

EFFIE: Hello? Yes, I'd like to talk to…who's in charge of uh…of uh…

WENDLE: Henry, we should get out of here in case the police get here with their guns out. Henry?

> *(HENRY looks at GRACE. She nods. HENRY and GRACE stand and walk out the door.)*

EFFIE: Well it's just that a couple of firecrackers went off in my house and I just wanted to tell them in case they…but I just want to tell them in case…

WENDLE: Alex. We should leave for a while. Alex.

EFFIE: Have you had a report of gunfire?

WENDLE: Come on. Alex. We have to go. We have to go now. Effie?

> *(WENDLE pulls ALEX towards the door.)*

EFFIE: But it was just a couple of firecrackers. I know but…but why. Okay… I understand but…but…

> *(Blackout. End of ACT III.)*

EPILOGUE

(Lights up. ALEX enters, pours himself a Scotch, sits on the couch. Bags of luggage at the base of the stairs. GRACE enters from the front door and goes upstairs. ALEX looks for the remote. He finds it, but does not turn the TV on. HENRY enters as GRACE walks down the stairs with EFFIE's stereo in a box.)

HENRY: You okay?

GRACE: Yeah.

(She struggles with it.)

ALEX: Henry, is the sound fixed?

HENRY: No, not yet.

GRACE: You could give us a fucking hand here.

(ALEX jumps up, and walks over and takes the box from GRACE. HENRY goes to EFFIE's room.)

HENRY: Actually I don't think there is anything left.

ALEX: I could help take the stuff to the car?

HENRY: The trunk's not open yet.

GRACE: Open it.

HENRY: Is that a command?

GRACE: It's not a command, but why do something halfway. Open the trunk so that we don't have to stop. You do things and then you don't finish them. It drives me crazy.

HENRY: Here.

              (HENRY gives the keys to ALEX and goes upstairs.)

ALEX: I'll go open the trunk.

              (ALEX leaves. WENDLE enters with some groceries. He goes to the kitchen. EFFIE walks down the stairs.)

EFFIE: Thanks a lot for helping me.

GRACE: No problem.

EFFIE: So call me tonight. We'll go out.

GRACE: Alright.

EFFIE: Promise?

GRACE: Promise.

EFFIE: No you won't.

GRACE: I will, I swear.

              (The phone rings. GRACE gets it.)

              Hello. Effie?

              (EFFIE shakes her head.)

              She's not in right now can I take a message? Okay. Right. Okay. Yes. Bye. That was your Mom. She wants you to call her with your new number.

EFFIE: I fuckin' gave it to her already. She's such a ditz.

              (ALEX returns.)

ALEX: Is all this stuff going too?

EFFIE: Actually, leave that. Henry?

HENRY: Yes?

EFFIE: Before we move anything, could you drive me to a hardware store? I have to get some keys copied before they close.

HENRY: Sure no problem.

(EFFIE hugs GRACE.)

ALEX: Well, see you later.

EFFIE: I'll be back in a half hour.

ALEX: But I might not be here when you get back so…

EFFIE: Alright. Well…alright.

(ALEX hugs her. She doesn't hug back. ALEX goes to the couch and turns on the TV.)

EFFIE: *(Calling.)* Goodbye Wendle.

WENDLE: What!

EFFIE: I'm heading out.

WENDLE: Alright.

EFFIE: Are you leaving in the next 20 minutes?

WENDLE: No.

EFFIE: Then I'll say goodbye when I come back.

WENDLE: Hey, fill your boots.

EFFIE: What?

WENDLE: Do what you have to do, I'll be here when you get back.

(EFFIE nods, grabs her purse and heads out the door.)

ALEX: Bye Henry.

HENRY: See you in a bit.

(HENRY blows GRACE a kiss and leaves. WENDLE goes to the backyard, reads a magazine. GRACE starts walking upstairs to her room. The phone rings. ALEX gets it.)

ALEX: Hello. Hello. Hello Kirk.

(GRACE stops.)

I think she's here. Hold on a second.

(GRACE takes the receiver. ALEX goes to the kitchen.)

GRACE: Hello? Hi. Yeah. I'm okay. How are you...where are you. I see. I see. No. Well, I feel that I want a second chance. Uh hunh, no but you see. Well...well if you think that's what's right for you... I said if you think that's right for you then I can't really argue can I. No I can't. Okay. Right. Well, it would be good if your stuff was gone by the end of the month because...because Henry is moving into your room. Yeah. Okay well the sooner the better. Right. Okay. Okay. Bye. Kirk... remember when Grandma stayed with us? It was the Easter just after you had the chicken pox. Yeah...and she would sit there watching television...an' she would take out her teeth and chew on the apples and spit out all the skin into a piece of tissue...and then she would get me to carry the skin to the garbage... Me. You lie... Oh Lord I can still remember the feel o dat mush in me hand. An' it all mix up wid de spit. *(She sucks her teeth.)* My hand drippin' wid it. You did not. Oh that is such a lie. That is such a lie. Anyway, I was just thinkin' about her yesterday, and I just thought I'd tell you. What?... Okay. Yes. Thank you for calling. Bye.

ALEX: What'd he say?

GRACE: He's fine.

ALEX: Where is he?

GRACE: Buffalo.

ALEX: Buffalo?

GRACE: Yeah.

               *(GRACE sits on the couch. ALEX looks to refill his
               drink but the bottle is empty.)*

ALEX: I remember when I was a kid, we had a big house,
               two car garage, big backyard, pool, barbecue, the
               whole bit. Some days when I was sick, or when
               there was a P.D. day or something, I would get to
               leave school early. And I would run home and my
               Nanny would be there to look after my little sister
               and she would have the ironing board set up right
               in front of the television, smoking her Craven A
               cigarettes eh, watching like... *Coronation Street* eh,
               or news reports about guerrillas hijacking planes
               to Cuba. And Pierre Trudeau was the coolest. We
               had no idea why, he just was, he was the coolest.
               And on those days when I was in a bad mood or
               something, I would go out into the backyard, and I
               would lay down on the grass and look up at the big
               blue sky and...and I'd just get these giggling fits
               right? 'Cause it would just strike me that Canada is
               so big. I mean, it's huge right? So I would jump up
               and try to see all the way over to Halifax but it was
               too far. Okay, so I'd jump up and try to see all the
               way over to Vancouver, but it was too far. Okay so
               I would stretch my arms out and try to touch the
               edge of Canada, but it was way too big. So I would
               flop on my stomach and grab fistfuls of grass and I
               would hug Canada. And you know what...if you
               stay really, really, really still, after a while, it almost
               feels like Canada is hugging you back. And I miss
               that feeling. I really do.

               *(He looks at her. He holds his arms out. She leans
               into his arms, he hugs her.)*

Shhh. Hey, Grace. Hey look. Look. See? We made CNN.

(Lights fade slowly.)

The End